THE SMALL
LANDLORD'S
GUIDE TO TENANT
SCREENING

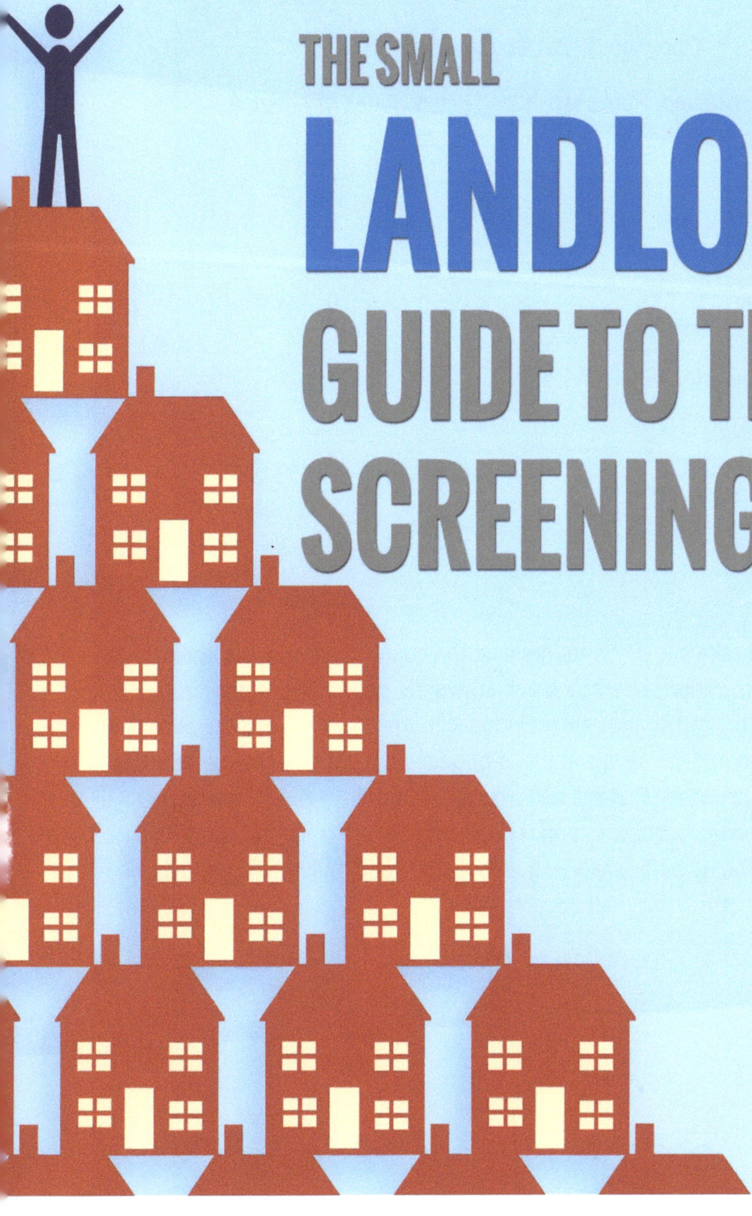

By VerticalRent.com

DISCLAIMER

Contents

Introducing: VerticalRent's Small Landlord's Guide to Tenant Screening

REVOLUTIONIZING THE INDUSTRY

VerticalRent was the first Web-based product for small landlords to introduce the direct-to-consumer tenant screening model coupled with online rent collection, vacancy advertising, financials, and tenant collaboration. It was built around the cornerstone of tenant screening. We believe that every small landlord deserves to have powerful tools available to effectively screen applicants and make smart leasing decisions. In this book, we are going to give every small landlord the knowledge needed to effectively screen applicants. But before we lay out the guide, let's give a little history to VerticalRent.

OUR ROOTS

The VerticalRent story started in 2005 in a one-bedroom apartment in Arlington, Virginia. Matt Angerer, a co-founder of VerticalRent, was talking to his dad on the phone about rental properties. John, Matt's dad, has been involved in the business of renting apartments for nearly 30 years and is still heavily involved until this day. John owns about 10 properties in Northwestern Pennsylvania and epitomizes how the average Joe can build a rental property portfolio over time. John and Cindy (Matt's mom), are now happily retired with cash flow from these rental properties, a 401k, and all the benefits social security can provide after retirement.

Flashback to 2005, when Matt was listening to his dad on the phone voice his frustration about tenants who trashed his apartments or wouldn't pay rent on time. The common themes from his tenants were: "the rent check is in the mail." Although Matt's dad was a firm believer in the power of rental properties to build wealth over time, he repeatedly told Matt, "It's a pain in the ass to be a small landlord, I'm telling you!" Naturally, the rent check would show up in his mailbox on the 6th or 7th of the month. This became a frustrating experience for John. Should he call the tenant on the 4th of the month if the check hasn't arrived yet? Or should he wait it out a few more days?

Matt listened to every frustrating word his dad spoke — a Small American Landlord. Late rent payments were a problem. The second issue was tenants who just didn't take care of his rental properties. They would put holes in the wall, rip up the carpets, and throw obscene parties. John was very meticulous about what he owned. And since his

rental properties were in close proximity to universities, he would often attract college students who would live in the house or apartment for a year and then move on — either graduating or off to the next apartment. Listening to his dad's frustrations, Matt considered whether or not he even wanted to get into the business of rental properties considering all the headaches it can cause. Naturally, it didn't deter him.

WHEN AMBITIONS FAR OUTWEIGH TALENT AND FUNDING

At the time, Matt was an IT consultant for the Defense Logistics Agency. He was making good money as a recent graduate of Penn State. Life was good. He didn't take the entrepreneurial path living out of a one-bedroom apartment with five other startup buddies. But a seed was planted in Matt's mind at an early age about the power of building wealth slowly with investment properties. Perhaps it was a combination of reading Robert Kiyosaki's book entitled "Rich Dad, Poor Dad" and listening to his own dad talk about his portfolio, or maybe it was a few chapters he read in "The Millionaire Next Door" — but Matt was determined to:

- ✅ Live the American Dream of Financial Freedom by being a Small American Landlord

- ✅ Build software tools that landlords could leverage

Step #1 was realized in 2006, when Matt purchased a foreclosed home for $59,000 USD in Erie, Pennsylvania. He fixed it up and rented it out. Step #2, however, took a backseat to his IT career and personal life. Although the seed was planted in his early 20s, the dream of building software to help small landlords wasn't fully realized until about five years later.

Fast forward to May 2011. Matt is now living in Westerville, Ohio, working for a global precision instruments company. He isn't much of a programmer, but he works in the IT industry. He continued to hear the frustration of small landlords and experienced it firsthand with a few "bad apples" renting from him. Convinced that the tenant screening industry needed an advanced Web-based product for small landlords, Matt set out to finally create one. He teamed up with a longtime friend to co-found VerticalCloud, the company behind VerticalRent. Both men worked tirelessly over a period of two years to launch VerticalRent.com. Within one year on the market, the product amassed nearly 5,000 small landlords from all 50 states. During this time period, Matt received feedback from thousands of small landlords.

"The Small Landlord's Guide to Tenant Screening" is the culmination of feedback Matt has received from VerticalRent customers, his experiences as a small landlord, and the lengthy process of designing, building, and rolling out VerticalRent software.

WHY SHOULD YOU EVEN CARE?

WHAT IS DIRECT TO CONSUMER TENANT SCREENING ANYHOW?

VerticalRent's direct-to-consumer tenant screening model makes it easy for small landlords to screen applicants. Direct-to-consumer simply means that the applicant (consumer) purchases and agrees to share their credit report with you first. As a landlord, you would use a product like VerticalRent.com to invite the applicant (via email or text) to share their credit report and online rental application with you. As part of the electronic rental application, you would then receive authorization to run a thorough criminal and eviction search on the applicant.

The convenience for consumers enables landlords like you to avoid the lengthy credentialing process, which often includes an onsite inspection and hefty setup fees. Many small landlords across the United States are members of local Apartment Associations. The landlords in Erie, Pennsylvania, where VerticalRent is currently headquartered, received a letter from the local Apartment Association mandating an onsite inspection. An onsite inspection?! Are you kidding me?! Most small landlords keep their paperwork in manila folders in a bedroom that serves as a quasi-office and grandma's room. But since many local Apartment Associations DO NOT involve the applicant in the process (other than a paper rental application with a wet signature), they are required to send someone out to the small landlord's house to check for things like a shredder, filing cabinet, and lock on the door.

Software products like VerticalRent.com and Experian Connect cater to small landlords and help keep you FCRA-compliant. The "checks and balances" mandated by the FCRA are built into the software workflow. In a nutshell, the applicant retrieves his or her own

credit report and then decides to share it with you, the landlord. You must first have permissible purpose and certify that you're looking at this applicant's credit report as part of the leasing process.

WHY READ THIS BOOK?

We aren't subtly plugging VerticalRent.com throughout this book. We make it very obvious from the start that VerticalRent.com and VerticalCloud are behind "The Small American Landlord" series of e-books. We have no shame in our game. What we do have is a burning desire to educate the estimated **40 million landlords** in the United States about important topics that will help them build wealth over the long term. We feel that a more educated American society, starting with Small American Landlords, will ultimately strengthen our economy. We believe in the powerful Small American Landlord and the tenants that they provide quality housing to on a monthly basis.

There is great potential for the aspiring investor seeking to purchase his or her first residential rental property or perhaps a few apartment buildings. Here are the main reasons you should read this book:

- ✅ This book is relatively short.

- ✅ You're a landlord who wants to protect his or her investment of time and money.

- ✅ The local Apartment Association hasn't fully stepped into the 21st century (just yet!).

- ✅ You own a smartphone (iPhone or Droid) and know how to use it.

- ✅ You've been burned a few times by "gut instinct" when choosing tenants.

- ✅ "I trust, but verify" isn't some line from a dead U.S. president — **it's now your motto.**

- ✅ Because the American Dream lives on within you!

WHY CAN YOU EXPECT FROM THIS BOOK?

Less grey hair? More hair? A Lamborghini?

Well, I guess we can't control our genetics, and Lamborghinis are overrated. Bald is beautiful, and pink is the new black — so get over it!

But what we can do for you is provide you with the knowledge, tools, and resources necessary to protect your rental property investment. We can give you a battle tested guide of how to approach tenant screening as a small landlord. Our hope is that this

e-book serves as an electronic reference to you for many years to come. When your small rental property empire is passed down to the next generation, we hope that you also provide this e-book as a reference to screening tenants.

When you're finished reading this guide, you will undoubtedly understand the power of:

- Retrieving **online rental apps and credit reports electronically**

- How to **avoid common background check traps** and get accurate results

- The **ONE key indicator** of an applicant's income vs. rent liability

- How to **confirm an applicant's identity** with a social security trace

- How to **objectively evaluate tenant screening providers**

- The Truth about checking references: **How to detect fake references**

- **Avoid the BIG Mistake** — What NOT to ask an applicant!

- Know what to ask prior landlords, **before you call**

- Verifying prior employment **with LinkedIn**

- **Vital ingredients** to establishing common criteria for evaluation

- Reasons why **one applicant is never enough — build a hopper!**

- How to keep it business-like with every applicant **(don't text and rent!)**

- **Proven and legal** ways to deny applicants without them making a fuss.

- A simple process that you can use today, tomorrow, and the day after.

Common Sense Ways to Screen

Most small landlords have experienced at least one issue with a problematic tenant. Whether it was a wild party that required the police to be summoned in order to quiet things down or involved chasing the tenant for overdue rent, such issues can be a hassle. Even more devastating is walking into a property recently vacated by a tenant only to discover that the unit is in disarray and expensive renovations are required. Such situations present the potential for lost income as a result of necessary repairs and the time required to complete those repairs. While these are certainly all nightmare scenarios, each could be minimized by conducting a thorough tenant check prior to renting a unit to a prospective tenant. By taking advantage of tenant screening services and checking the background of an applicant, the risk of such scenarios becomes much lower. Not only do bad tenants cost you money, but their actions can also result in potential liabilities. There are three ways in which you can conduct a tenant check.

THE TELEPHONE INTERVIEW

Most likely, the first contact you will often have with a tenant is over the telephone. Even if you are using an online rental application, the first time you actually speak to the applicant will often be over the phone. This is an excellent opportunity to ask questions to initiate the qualification process. Along with gathering the applicant's name and contact number, you should also ask if the applicant has landlord references. Other questions to ask include:

REASON FOR MOVING?

Sounds crazy, but you will get a sense if they are fleeing from somewhere. Not to worry, though, you can check both state and national criminal records for transient applicants from different parts of the United States.

It's been our experience that some applicants omit the entire truth with this question, especially college students. You should be firm about your occupant limit with the house. We have seen applicants sublet rooms out. The issue with this type of arrangement with your knowledge is that you can't pursue the other individuals in the court of law unless they are a named individual on the lease agreement. Lease agreements are another topic in the "Small American Landlord" series, though. For now, we advise that you emphasize the importance of announcing all occupants that plan to live in the rental property.

NUMBER OF PEOPLE WHO WILL OCCUPY THE UNIT

TYPE AND NUMBER OF PETS, IF APPLICABLE

There isn't a universal opinion from the Small American Landlord in allowing pets. Our suggestion is to probe the applicant on the phone as to the type of pet. Is it a dog? How big is the dog? How long have you owned it? The reason we suggest staying flexible on the pet rule is because there are millions of applicants with pets who get turned down right away just because they own a pet. This is your opportunity as a small landlord to secure a long-term tenant. Animal loving tenants know that many landlords don't accept pets. If you're smart about things — you can charge the applicant a nonrefundable pet deposit. Worst case scenario is that the dog defecates all over your residential rental house. If you collected a $300 nonrefundable pet deposit and also a security deposit, you should have no issues cleaning up the mess. The bottom line is not to be so anxious about renting to tenants with pets. Just be smart about it. Don't rent to someone with four German shepherds when the house is 1,100 square feet. Use your common sense!

In addition to asking the questions above, you should inform the applicant of the rent amount, security deposit, and any other fees required upfront, like the nonrefundable pet security deposit. This helps set the stage and expectations upfront with the applicant. You should also use this as an opportunity to establish yourself as a Small American

Landlord and not their "buddy." Many applicants want to be your "buddy" when they call about a place. Some will even try to negotiate on the rent. Our suggestion to you is to interact with every applicant in a **consistent and methodical manner**.

Don't use slang. Watch your language. If you're a construction worker by trade and drop the "F" bomb in every other sentence, try to clean up your approach when you speak to applicants. If you find yourself of the same age as the applicant or perhaps a little younger, don't let this be an excuse to get "too friendly" with them. If you're renting to college students, they might try to joke around with you about inviting you out to a keg party. Our suggestion is to laugh off comments like that and keep "the power distance."

The Power Distance is a term used in corporate America with managers and team leads. The same principles apply with the Small American Landlord. Get too friendly, and people try to take advantage. Maintain the power distance at all times, with every interaction. Keep it strictly business-like when engaging with a potential tenant and also current tenants. And finally, if an applicant or tenant is "text happy" — follow these rules about SMS texting:

✓ You can exchange texts with an applicant or tenant in a controlled fashion. What we mean by a "controlled fashion" is that you keep it short and to the point. The same principle applies with email communication. You never want to put yourself into a situation where something could be misconstrued with an applicant or tenant. There are Fair Housing Laws (to be discussed later), and any small slip in communication could result in hefty fines.

✓ Never reply to text messages after 9 p.m. unless it's a maintenance emergency. There are reasons for this rule around texting that will be discussed in a later series of the "Small American Landlord." For now, just be careful with texting and email communication. Pick up the phone and call them. Keep it short, concise, and to the point. Business-like.

PERSONAL FACE-TO-FACE INTERVIEW

If you and the applicant are satisfied after the telephone interview, you may choose to schedule a time for the applicant to tour the rental property. This visit also affords you the perfect opportunity to continue the qualification process. There is much information that can be gleaned from a personal interview. Once again, you have to be careful about what you say to a potential renter. A few things you can ask and also observe are:

✓ Ask the applicant about his or her prior renting history and whether he or she can fill out a rental application. In the same breath, ask how the applicant heard about the property and whether he or she already submitted an online rental application.

✓ If an applicant hasn't submitted an online rental application, observe whether he or she carries a smartphone. Most people these days are carrying a smartphone. Ask the applicant if he or she has heard of AppSingular (www.appsingular.com) and explain that the applicant can submit the rental application directly to you from that Web-based service. Hand over a business card with your QR code on the back. The applicant can quickly scan the QR code and complete the rental application while walking through the property or when he or she gets home. As a VerticalRent.com customer, you have a unique QR code for your online rental application. You can print this off on fliers or put it on the back of a business card. Most Small American Landlords carry around a business card with their QR code on the back.

FORMAL TENANT SCREENING – WHAT THIS BOOK IS ALL ABOUT!

Keep in mind that all of the information obtained through the application, telephone interview, and personal interview should be confirmed with a formal tenant check. Tenant screening services, such as VerticalRent, can help you in performing a credit check as well as a criminal background check. You will need to obtain the applicant's online rental application in order to pull a criminal and eviction check. Once the applicant completes the online rental application with AppSingular, he or she is asked to digitally sign off on the application before sharing it with you. At this point, you have full authority to run a criminal and eviction search on the applicant and use these as decision markers.

These checks are vital, as they can reveal a wealth of information that the applicant may not volunteer on his or her own. For instance, a credit check will tell you whether the applicant pays his or her bills on time. Additionally, a credit check will reveal debt load, collections, bankruptcies, evictions, and judgments. Criminal history data will reveal any adjudications and charges as well as their outcome. You can also use a criminal background check to verify the applicant's identify along with any aliases.

WHY YOU CAN'T AFFORD TO SKIP A TENANT CHECK

When it comes to renting your property, it is important to know who will be residing in your unit. A comprehensive tenant check can provide you with the information you need to make an informed decision about who will occupy your property.

Without a proper tenant screening, it can be easy to run into trouble. Tenants may not pay their rent on time or could refuse to pay for damage they cause in your unit. Unruly tenants can also create disturbances in the neighborhood and become a nuisance to other tenants. In order to avoid such conflicts, it is important to ensure that you evaluate potential tenants.

MORE EFFICIENT OPERATIONS

One of the most common reasons that many small landlords give for not conducting a tenant check is simply not having the time or resources to do so. Being a small landlord can be time-consuming. When you need to rent a unit quickly, it is completely natural to want to skip over some steps and simply go with your gut instinct. While this might work out well some of the time, it is a risk that can cost you even more time and money in the long run. Conducting a professional tenant check can assist you in screening your tenants while saving effort and time.

CREDITWORTHINESS

As a small landlord, you have a responsibility to run a tenant check on potential tenants prior to signing a lease agreement. Doing so will eliminate any doubt regarding the tenant's ability to pay the rent. Additionally, a tenant check will provide some insight into the type of tenant the applicant may be and whether the applicant is suitable for your unit. With a professional tenant check, you do not have to worry about taking time out of your schedule to perform a background check. The tenant screening service will conduct a thorough background check on the applicants for you and then provide any relevant information you might need to know.

CRIMINAL BACKGROUND CHECKS

If you have encountered a situation where an applicant is referred to you by a friend, family member, or even another tenant, you may feel awkward about running a background check to obtain necessary information regarding the tenant's background. Failure to run the proper background check can lead to even more problems later on. In order to avoid such problems, it is advisable to have a tenant screening service do the job for you. This will help to remove the burden from your shoulders while still helping you to make an informed decision. As a small landlord, you need to know if a tenant may use your property in an illegal manner or even if he or she has ever been convicted for any unlawful activity in the past.

Managing a property rental business comes with numerous responsibilities. Among those responsibilities is ensuring that you rent to reliable, creditworthy tenants.

BENEFITS OF AN ONLINE RENTAL APPLICATION

The property rental business has dramatically changed in the last few years. Among the most significant changes is the transition to online management. As a small landlord, you must make the transition to an online or electronic rental application for a few reasons:

IT'S QUICK AND EFFECTIVE

Whether you have one property or dozens of properties, you need a system for organizing applications that is fast and efficient. An online rental application is an excellent solution. By handling as much of your work online as possible, you can manage your property rental business in a much faster and more efficient manner. You also gain the ability to track the status of each application, make notes, and instantly communicate application status with your tenants.

INCREASED BUSINESS

You might be surprised to find that an online rental application can actually help you to generate more interest in your units. Tenants, particularly younger tenants, are more likely to inquire about online rental applications. The simple fact of the matter is that potential tenants are more likely to rent from you if you provide an online rental application option. In addition to eliminating the need to complete paperwork, an online rental application option also removes the need for prospective tenants to actually drive to your office. Ultimately, offering an online application makes life easier for your tenants, and the easier you can make the application process, the more likely tenants are to actually rent your unit.

MORE TENANTS TO CHOOSE FROM

The last thing you want is to be stuck in a situation where you feel as though you must rent a unit to a questionable tenant because there is no one else. With an online rental application, you will have more prospective tenants, giving you the opportunity to select the most reliable tenants. As you already know, reliable tenants are a key ingredient to a profitable property rental business. With an online rental application, you remove the guesswork from finding quality tenants by ensuring that you have the best information for making an informed decision while ensuring you are in compliance.

ENSURE COMPLIANCE

Making certain that you are in compliance with the leasing regulations for your state can be time-consuming and a hassle. By opting to take advantage of an online rental application, you can set aside those worries. State-specific rental applications ensure that you are completely covered and in compliance.

TAKE ADVANTAGE OF ONLINE SHARING

With the option to embed an Apply Now button on most rental vacancy ads, you can embed the rental application on your Facebook or website for increased exposure.

Paper rental applications have rapidly become a thing of the past. An increasing number of tenants are now actively requesting online rental application options. In addition to helping you operate your property business more quickly, online rental applications also help you to tap into a larger market and ensure that you remain compliant.

SIGNIFICANT COST SAVINGS

Many brokers and landlords are still driving to their rentals with a clipboard and paper rental applications. Applicants fill out lengthy rental applications, and the landlord is tasked with re-entering this information into a spreadsheet or scanning it into a computer. Over the last few years, technology has advanced to the point where this is no longer necessary.

Do you realize that you are actually losing money by using a clipboard and paper rental applications? Let's take a look at the "true cost" of not converting to an online rental application:

$

EXTRA GAS COST

every time you drive out to visit an applicant for a walk-thru, you are putting wear and tear on your vehicle and burning gas. Many times, the applicants do not even qualify for the rental property and you don't know that until after the fact. By using an online rental application, you can prequalify the applicants before wasting your time driving out there for a dead lead.

If you're still using paper rental applications and retyping this information into a lease agreement after accepting an applicant, you're wasting your time. Most Apartment Associations through the United States will give you a stack of paper rental applications. A lot of Small American Landlords are collecting information on these paper rental applications and driving them down to the Apartment Association office. The service they offer is certainly valuable, we will not discount that; however — look at how much time you are wasting by doing this. With an online rental application, you receive the necessary authorization to retrieve a credit, criminal, and eviction report — electronically. What's more is that you can quickly convert this online rental application into a state-specific lease agreement with a few clicks.

EXTRA COST OF TIME SPENT RETYPING INFORMATION

COST OF ORGANIZATION

Think about your filing cabinets, folders, and space taken up at home or in the office with filing paperwork. There is cost associated with every aspect of organizing paperwork. Going paperless gives you the ability to auto-organize your electronic rental applications.

This is an obvious cost to going paperless with online rental applications, but think about how much you're spending yearly on paper and ink. If you go to Wal-Mart or Target and look at how much HP is charging for ink, it's enough to make you go paperless today!

COST OF PAPER AND INK/TONER

COST OF REPETITION

Cost of repetition — how much time is it taking you to file paperwork, make copies, and scan/attach to emails? With VerticalRent, you eliminate the overhead involved with the tedious administrative tasks.

Now take a moment to consider the glaring benefits of going paperless with online rental applications:

✓ By prequalifying applicants, you're putting less wear and tear on your vehicle as a small landlord. You don't have to run over to the rental after work to collect a few paper rental apps. Add the "Apply Now" button to your website and allow applicants to apply electronically. Filter them out quickly while you're at the office!

✓ Each incoming rental application is automatically named, organized, and digitally stored in its proper place!

✓ You're cutting down on extra paper use and spending less money on ink/toner. What's more is that you're doing your small part as a landlord to help out the environment.

![American flag, Constitution "We the People", and the U.S. Capitol building]

REJECTING AN APPLICANT

It's inevitable that you will need to reject a few applicants. In fact, if you're screening applicants correctly — you'll be rejecting a batch of applicants during each leasing cycle. Never make a decision off one rental application. We recommend collecting at least five rental apps before deciding on an applicant. There can be a number of reasons why you might reject a rental application. Perhaps there are concerns from the applicant's background or credit check. Maybe the number of people listed on an application exceeds the unit's maximum occupancy. Or, maybe he or she has a pet when you have a strict no-pet policy. Whatever the case may be, when you need to reject a rental applicant, you need to know how to do it without opening yourself up to liability.

No one ever wants to hear the word no. Unfortunately, when you are a landlord and you tell a tenant no, unless you are able to demonstrate that you have followed Fair Housing laws, that no could result in fines and litigation. In order to maintain your business, you need to know how to protect yourself. Following the tips below can help to guide you in this matter. These tips should not be construed as legal advice. You should always consult with your attorney for legal advice on rejecting a rental application.

BE HONEST

First and foremost, it is important that you be upfront and honest regarding the reason for issuing the rejection. There is sometimes a tendency to try to ease a rejection by beating around the bush. Although it is commendable that you might not want to hurt an applicant's feelings, for your own protection, you need to provide him or her with the real reason for the rejection. Not only will this protect you, but it will also help the applicant to understand the situation so he or she can make improvements when applying for other rentals in the future.

DEALING WITH CREDIT REPORTS

One of the most common reasons for rejecting a rental application relates to issues with credit reports. When this is the case, you are legally bound to inform applicants of this. Not only must you tell them that their credit was the problem, but you must also provide them with the name of the credit reporting agency that gave you the relevant information. VerticalRent.com is considered a consumer reporting agency (CRA) in the eyes of the FCRA. If you're rejecting an applicant based on a credit report received on VerticalRent. com, you can provide the applicant with an automated adverse action notice that will clearly provide our contact information if the consumer wants to see a copy of the credit report. This will allow the applicant to dispute the relevant credit report, if he or she wishes to do so. Keep in mind that in order to protect yourself, you must use the same credit guidelines for all applicants. **Do not make exceptions.**

DOCUMENTATION IS KING

Before you even consider issuing a rejection, make certain that the applicant in question has signed the necessary authorization for you to complete a background check. This should include providing permission for a credit check to be performed and for references listed on the application to be contacted.

Make certain that you keep documentation of any and all contact you have with the applicant in question. This is an excellent way to prove that you did not violate the law in any way when you must issue a rejection.

Rejecting an applicant is never pleasant or easy. It is, however, part of the job. Understanding how to do it without leaving yourself liable for legal action is critical.

UNDERSTANDING CRIMINAL RECORDS

As a small landlord, it is only natural for you to want to know more about an applicant before deciding to rent your property to that person. In order to avoid accidentally renting your property to an undesirable tenant, a criminal background check can provide you with the information you need to make an informed decision. This type of check is completely lawful and can include a wealth of information about your applicant, including personal information, lawsuit history, and criminal history. Ultimately, this information can assist you in determining the applicant's trustworthiness.

In most instances, a criminal record will include any criminal offenses that have not been expunged from the individual's record. As such, it will also typically include traffic offenses, including drunk driving and speeding.

In the event that the individual has been arrested, the report will contain an explanation of the end result, including any convictions and sentences that were received. Not guilty verdicts, dismissals, and bench warrant statuses will also be listed. Any alias names and probation or parole violations will be noted on the report, as well. In addition, the report will include any differences regarding the individual's dates of birth or social security numbers that have been used.

Criminal records are maintained in the United States by law enforcement agencies by every level of government, ranging from the federal government to local sheriffs' departments and police departments. Law enforcement agencies will typically share this type of information with other agencies. In addition, this information will often be made available to the public.

In most instances, the only group that is not subjected to the release of criminal information is juveniles. Nondisclosure of criminal information may also be required in the case of some adults in the event that records have been sealed or the record has been expunged.

In some states, there are repositories where criminal record information is contributed by courts throughout that state. Such repositories are typically quite accurate provided that

they are supervised. Reporting and supervision may only be voluntary in some states, however. As a result, information contained from such repositories could potentially be incomplete. In addition, the federal government also maintains its own criminal history repository that is quite extensive. The National Crime Information Center (NCIC) typically does not make its records available to the public.

At VerticalRent, we provide comprehensive criminal record searches. As a landlord, it is imperative that you make a point of understanding your own local state laws and ensure that you follow them accordingly when requesting criminal record searches. You should also be aware of your legal responsibilities regarding the notification of applicants if you decide to decline a rental application. Additionally, you should be aware of any exceptions that may apply that might prohibit you from turning down an applicant based on the information in the report. While most consumer reporting agencies scrub data, as do we, it should be understood that such agencies are not able to guarantee the accuracy of the data.

TOP 10 REASONS TO SCREEN APPLICANTS

Many small landlords roll the dice when it comes to filling their vacancies. They post an ad, collect a few paper rental applications, and rent it to the first person who comes to the table with the security deposit. Legally screening tenants involves asking for a legitimate rental application, a credit report, verifying prior landlords, and also running a state and national criminal + eviction report on the prospective tenant. Here are the Top 10 Reasons to Screen Applicants compiled by The Small American Landlord:

1
HISTORY OFTEN REPEATS ITSELF WITH RENTERS

Don't roll the dice or give up the keys to your investment properties without properly investigating a prospective tenant. A "proper investigation" is subjective, but we're fanatics about helping you analyze risk and reward. The reward is a good tenant who pays rent on time and doesn't damage your property. The risk is a bad tenant who damages your property and doesn't pay rent. VerticalRent's historical credit, criminal, and eviction reports help you pinpoint problem tenants quickly **and weed them out**!

2
LIABILITY

With VerticalRent, you have a secure and electronic audit trail with your current, prospective, and past tenants — starting with the initial rental application, powered by AppSingular. If one of your tenants engages in illegal activities on the premise of your investment property, having the screening results on file can protect you from liability.

3
PROTECTING FAMILY INHERITANCE

Small landlords aren't doing it for their health. They are building a nest egg for their family and hopefully a secure retirement. Screening applicants is necessary to ensure the family inheritance is protected.

4
PROPERTY DAMAGE

With a background investigation, you will know whether a previous landlord has tried to sue a prospective tenant for damaging property.

5
AVOIDING SQUATTERS

Our online rental application, powered by AppSingular, allows you to quickly weed out prospective tenants who have squatted in an apartment. Evicting a tenant, although not overly complicated, does take a little bit of time. Asking the right questions on a formal rental application legally binds the tenant to answering the online tenant application truthfully.

6
KNOWING WHO BREAKS LEASES

You want stable renters who live up to the commitment of their lease agreements.

7
MOVED WHILE OWING A LANDLORD RENT

It happens all of the time in college towns. Local professionals buy up a few apartment buildings and build a secondary revenue stream with the influx of college students who rent from them. The unfortunate news is that most of these college students are not local and will often skip rent toward the end of a semester. Since history often repeats itself with renters, you will know if they have done this in the past.

8
REFERENCES

Beyond landlord references, your tenant can authorize you to contract neighbors, employers, credit bureaus, creditors, and all other individuals necessary to perform a thorough and investigative screening. Your online rental application, powered by AppSingular, ensures that you have the authorization to do so.

9
OTHER OCCUPANTS

You should always know which other occupants will be living with a tenant in your dwelling. An online rental application, powered by AppSingular, will allow you to screen the other occupants — not just the primary on the lease agreement. You can also enable online rent collection for each tenant living in the dwelling — allowing each to pay this or her share of the rent individually through an online portal.

10
PEACE OF MIND

Everyone has varying tolerances for risk. Enough said.

ESTABLISHING VALID CRITERIA FOR SELECTING APPLICANTS

Establishing tenant selection criteria can be one of the most confusing areas of operating rental property for many people. On one hand, you want to make sure you choose the most responsible tenant possible; a tenant who will pay his or her rent on time and one who can be relied upon not to destroy your property. Yet, at the same time, you must make sure that you abide by Fair Housing laws.

Before you actually begin renting out your property, it is a good idea to sit down and determine the criteria you will use to choose that best tenant. Without guidelines, you will have no choice but to rely on your instinct to choose the best tenant, and this could result in trouble if you are only relying on your feelings to make a tenant selection. One of the worst risks you can take is to let your own personal opinions and biases guide you in your decision, because this could open the door for a discrimination lawsuit.

First, you should always make sure that you notify prospective tenants that you utilize a fair system to make your decision. Ideally, it is best to include this type of statement on all rental applications. For example, you might state "Our policy is to rent our units in compliance with federal, state, and local fair housing laws."

If you are fairly new to operating investment rental property, you may not be cognizant of fair housing laws. Be sure to consult your state's fair housing office to determine those guidelines, which you must follow. Beyond fair housing laws, it is important to make sure you establish criteria that is concrete by which to judge all potential applicants.

For example, it is common to require that the applicant provide identification that is verifiable. You may require the applicant to present a photo ID with the application so

that you can make a copy of it. This type of requirement is valid, because you may need it in the future in the event you need to describe adult occupants of the unit. If someone co-signs the application, it is also a good idea to obtain identification for the co-signer as well.

It is also quite valid to require information that would help you to determine that the applicant has a sufficient income-to-rent ratio. If the applicant were applying for a loan to purchase a home, the lender would require similar information. **The general rule of thumb is to identify applicants that have a gross monthly income that is three times the amount of the rent.** One way to document this information is by requesting copies of the applicant's pay stubs along with the application. AppSingular allows applicants to upload scanned digital copies of their paystubs and other information to verify income. If the applicant is self-employed, you might ask him or her to provide the last tax return in addition to three months of bank statements. If you cannot verify the applicant's income, this would be a perfectly legitimate reason to deny an application, as you have no assurance that he or she would be able to pay rent.

As you know, we encourage every small landlord to check credit, criminal, eviction, and references on applicants. The purpose of this is to verify the financial responsibility of the applicant, character, prior renting history, and what prior landlords and employers reveal about him or her. The general guideline is to obtain a credit report on all applicants as well as any co-signers who are over the age of 18. Keep in mind that you will need to receive permission to run a criminal and eviction search; however, the online rental application you receive through AppSingular already contains the authorization. Applicants with low credit scores could be legitimately denied on the basis on being unable to prove financial responsibility. But what is considered a good credit score? Let's first explain the VantageScore model.

The credit report small landlords receive through VerticalRent includes the VantageScore calculation. It's different than the FICO score and much better, in our opinion. The VantageScore calculation was developed by the three national credit reporting companies – Experian, TransUnion, and Equifax. Unlike the other scoring systems, VantageScore is the most consistent score using only one model with one set of scoring calculations, resulting in scores that are more uniform and consistent. Ultimately, this provides landlords with assurance that this ONE SCORE is accurate. You don't need to worry about getting a credit report from all three credit reporting agencies. If you're viewing the VantageScore – you can rest easy knowing that all three credit-reporting agencies weighed into the score.

More specifically, VerticalRent leverages VantageScore 3.0. This model combines better performing analytics with more granular data from the three national credit reporting companies. What are the benefits of using VerticalRent's score to make a decision?

✅ The score is **more predictive** because it uses the most granular data.

✅ The score is the **most consistent,** thanks to a unique and patented characteristic leveling process.

✅ The score is **more inclusive**, scoring up to <u>35 million previously unscoreable consumers</u>. Many applicants that once didn't have a credit score now do with our model.

✅ The score is **more stable** — accounting for changes in consumer behavior.

✅ The score is **more user-friendly**. It's simple for **small landlords** to understand.

✅ The score is **more accurate**. It's based on <u>post-recession data</u>.

✅ The score is **more familiar**. It uses a score range of **300 to 850**.

There is no single set of "good" or "bad" VantageScore credit scores, unfortunately. Every small landlord tolerates risk somewhat differently and establishes his or her own "cutoffs" based on acceptable risk. For example, you may decide to collect two months of security deposit for a VantageScore below 600 and only one month of security deposit for a VantageScore above 600. The additional month of security deposit collected upfront mitigates the risk of a lower VantageScore. Mortgage lenders often establish internal criteria themselves when reviewing home applicant loans. Here is a quick breakdown of the scoring factors that VerticalRent's VantageScore 3.0 takes into account:

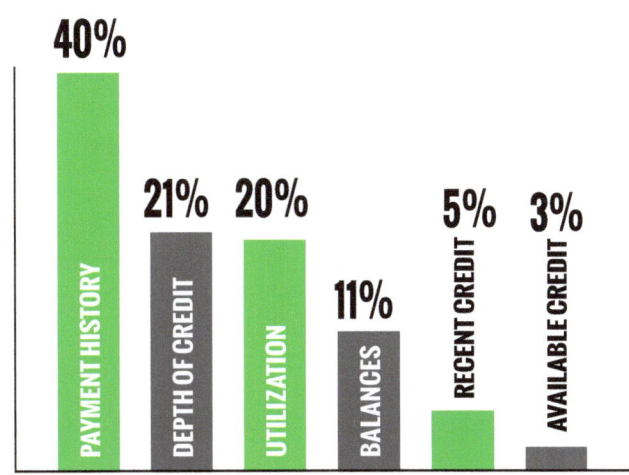

According to Fitch Ratings and Standard & Poor's, the VantageScore 3.0 is used by:

The Small American Landlord recommends the following guidelines for varying "risk profiles":

- ✓ Ultra-conservative small landlords should require a VantageScore of 760 or higher as their cutoff point. If all of your applicants come in below 760, then you should pick the highest and require 2 months of security deposit upfront.

- ✓ Conservative small landlords should require a VantageScore of 720 or higher.

- ✓ Most small landlords are safe accepting a VantageScore of 700 or higher.

- ✓ Anything below 650 is suspect and falls below the average American credit score. Every landlord has varying levels of risk. You can rent to someone with a VantageScore of 600 and receive rent on time every month. On the other hand, you could rent to someone with a VantageScore of 800 and he or she could run into financial difficulties for the first time while leasing from you. It's a gamble either way. The key is to mitigate risk and make informed decisions.

In addition, you should check references. Typically, you should ask all applicants to provide the names and telephone numbers of individuals who can verify the applicant's income sources as well as character references. Most young professionals are using LinkedIn these days. You can verify employment by viewing their public LinkedIn profile as a double-measure.

Finally, make sure you follow up to check that the applicant has been able to successfully rent a dwelling in the past and paid rent on time. In the event an applicant is unable to meet this requirement but does meet all other requirements, you may consider requiring the applicant to have a co-signer.

Evaluating Applicant Income

Evaluating applicant income can be tricky if you're not asking for the right information. Many tenant screening providers provide a recommendation service for landlords. At Small American Landlord, we think this can be valuable for some landlords — *but it doesn't take a rocket scientist to review a few key indicators on the tenant application and make a decision.* What concerns us about the "recommendation service" offered by some of the Web-based tenant screening providers on the market is that errors can always exist in the system logic to generate this recommendation. If a landlord is blindly flipping through digital apps and only looking at the recommendation provided, he or she could easily make a mistake and put the keys in the wrong hands.

Here are a few things we encourage landlords to review:

A rule of thumb: What we recommend for evaluating income vs. rent is similar to what financial gurus recommend, and that is to ensure the rent price does not exceed 30 percent of the applicant's overall income.

Generally, an applicant's income should be approximately three to four times the amount of the rent.

Prescreening Your Applicants

Taking the time to prescreen applicants can actually help to save you a tremendous amount of time later on and weed out undesirable applicants. The prescreening process begins with your first contact with the applicant. In most instances, this will be over the telephone, but it could also be through email or some other medium. The goal of prescreening is to determine whether there is even a point in proceeding to the next step of the process. Usually, the best way to determine whether a tenant is qualified to go on to the next step is to advise him or her of the upfront rent and security deposit requirements as well as any other important facts related to the rental. You may well find that the applicant says, "OK, thanks," and hangs up the phone. And, if that is what happens, that's fine. It's better to find out at this point that applicants cannot afford the rent than to waste your time meeting with them, showing them the property, and then discovering that they can't afford it.

Remember, your time is valuable, too. Additionally, by conducting a pre-interview, you are also actually saving your applicants time. It's better for them to know upfront that this isn't the rental for them rather than having them waste their time meeting with you in person only to be told that they do not qualify.

It's a good idea to have a list of questions handy to ask prospects when you are conducting a first contact interview. Such questions include the basics:

- ✅ Name

- ✅ Reason for moving

- ✅ Intended rental term

- ✅ Telephone number

✓ Number of people to live in the unit and their relationship to the applicant

✓ Desired occupancy date

✓ Smoking

✓ Pets

Take note that any applicant who has problems answering these basic questions probably will not qualify for your rental. Serious applicants want to make a good impression and should be happy to answer your questions.

Prohibited Questions

The goal of interviewing prospective tenants is to ensure that you get the best tenant for your rental property. Consequently, you naturally will want to ask as many questions as possible to ensure they are an ideal candidate. With that said, you must exercise caution. There are actually many questions that you are not legally allowed to ask.

QUESTIONS IN VIOLATION OF FAIR HOUSING LAWS

You must never ask any questions that could be construed as discrimination under the Federal Fair Housing Law or your state's fair housing law. Keep in mind that seven classes are protected under the Federal Fair Housing Act. They are: race, religion, color, national origin, sex, familial status, and disability. Additionally, many states have also elected to add additional protected classes, such as sexual orientation and marital status.

QUESTIONS OUT OF THE NORM

When screening prospective tenants, it is vital to ensure that you treat all applicants in a consistent manner. Failure to do so can put you at risk for a discrimination suit. Therefore, it is imperative that you have the same qualifying standards for all applicants. For instance, you have the legal right to perform credit checks on all applicants provided that they consent to a credit check. But, if you only perform credit checks on minority applicants, this would be considered discriminatory. The same holds true if you only ask applicants who may not be dressed well about their criminal convictions or eviction history, but you do not pose those same questions to applicants that you consider to be well dressed. To avoid any hint of discriminatory treatment, make sure that you ask all applicants the same questions.

Remember, avoid asking questions that relate to any of the following topics:

- ✓ Race, national origin, color, gender, or ancestry
- ✓ Age
- ✓ Sexual orientation
- ✓ Religion
- ✓ Marital status
- ✓ Military/veteran status
- ✓ Children
- ✓ Disability
- ✓ Receipt of public assistance

Questions to Ask Employers and Prior Landlords

If an applicant meets the prescreening process, he or she will then advance to the next phase, which includes you contacting both employers and prior landlords. This is another area that many small landlords are often tempted to skip because it can take time. After all, if you have verified prospective tenants' income through check stubs and you have vetted them with an application, why bother calling up their employers and prior landlords? The reason is that regardless of how good an applicant may look on paper, he or she can still have some skeletons lurking in the closet, so to speak. Suppose an applicant provided you with a copy of his or her last paystub but neglected to mention that he or she was just fired after receiving that last pay stub? How can you be sure that a tenant wasn't actually evicted from his or her last rental? The only way to know for certain is to follow up. Furthermore, if a tenant will lie about something related to employment or prior rentals, even if it seems inconsequential, there is really no telling what else he or she might lie about.

Questions to Ask Prior Landlords

✓ Did the previous tenant pay the rent?

✓ Did he or she pay it on time?

✓ Did he or she do a reasonably good job of taking care of the rental property?

✓ Was the unit clean and in good order when this tenant left?

✓ Was this person disruptive toward other tenants or neighbors?

✓ Did the tenant communicate well?

✓ Would you rent to this tenant again?

Questions to Ask Employers

✓ Is/was this person employed by you?

✓ How long has this person been employed by you?

✓ Can you confirm the income provided by the applicant?

Glossary of Landlord Terms

Part of the process of developing a successful rental property business is ensuring you understand the lingo commonly used. Below, you will find terms and definitions that you will commonly encounter in the business.

LANDLORD
A person or entity that rents or leases property to an organization or another person. A landlord has certain responsibilities to the tenant through a rental agreement and which is specified by law.

TENANT
An entity or person that leases property from another. By paying rent, the tenant has limited use of the property and rights of possession for a specified time, usually per a written lease. The tenant is responsible for abiding by the terms of the lease.

LEASE
A contract, typically written, with a certain duration allowing a tenant to occupy or use a property subject to the terms of the contract.

SUBLEASE
A rental agreement between the tenant and a third party that allows the third party, known as the sub lessee, to use the property for a specified time. Also known as sublet.

EVICTION
A judicial or legal process by which a landlord forces a tenant to vacant a rental property and by which the rental agreement is terminated for failure to follow the terms of the agreement.

TENANCY
The period during which a tenant has the right to use and possess a rental property.

FORCIBLE ENTRY
Entry by a landlord into a leased property without prior consent of the tenant.

NUISANCE
Any activity or conduct by a tenant that is so egregious in nature that it interferes with the safety or health of other tenants or people within the community.

FAIR HOUSING ACT
The Fair Housing Act, part of Title VIII of the Civil Rights Act of 1968, which was enacted to eliminate discrimination and bias in home sales and renting on the basis of an individual's personal characteristics, such as creed, religion, race, gender, national origin, disability, or family status.

www.ingramcontent.com/pod-product-compliance
Lightning Source LLC
Chambersburg PA
CBHW041151180526
45159CB00002BB/775